Frozen Charlotte

THE BREADTH OF SUSAN DE SOLA'S POETRY, by turns gossamer light and solemnly elegiac, offers a pleasurable aesthetic surprise from poem to poem—from "sun-starved Dutchmen" to immigrant Jews in Manhattan, from tulips to the life of a friend whose actual name she never knew, from the imagined language of rocks to a war widow's cedar closet, from the death of an infant to conjugal love. Susan de Sola evinces wit and knowingness, a dexterity with verse, a way with form. But more important is to understand the human heart. Its secrets transcend all of wit's cunning. And the pleasure of de Sola's poetry is to be in the presence of virtuosity and insight, of a poet who knows what it means to be human, and when to be serious and when to be light.

—Mark Jarman, author of *The Heronry*

WHEN I READ SUSAN DE SOLA'S UNCANNY TITLE POEM "Frozen Charlotte" for the first time, I couldn't stop thinking about it. I feel the same about the book as a whole, a virtuoso grouping of form and topic, a book that is haunting, yet which also sparkles with a sense of humor that I much enjoyed. Susan de Sola, it seems, can write in any form. While this book is her first full-length collection, it is the work of a master craftsperson.

—Kim Bridgford, author of *Undone*

WHETHER THEIR SUBJECT IS A PAINTING by Sargent, a gathering at the site of a Holocaust deportation center, or the bestial appearance of ATM machines, Susan de Sola's poems seem animate with her vision: the poems breathe on the page. Part of de Sola's power lies in her formal acumen. Every word here seems carefully sieved from the welter of English, and each poem's form is perfectly matched to its ambition and music. De Sola's tonal range is equally rich—she is by turns funny and dark, pensive and sly, her voice resounding in the reader's head long after a poem's final line. I will not forget the suite of animal poems here, or the poet's moving meditation on the death of an infant, or her description of the stuff atop the bureau of her teenage son, an inventory both tender and hilarious. Like its memorable title poem, *Frozen Charlotte* intrigues, goes deep, surprises. It is a book rich with the pleasures the best poetry provides.
　　—Clare Rossini, author of *Lingo*

THIS BOOK HAS MANY MOODS AND MANY MESSAGES for any reader who pays the poems collected here the attention they deserve. At times it seems a fairground, at times a graveyard, and neither cancels the other out. It is a mark of Susan de Sola's always persuasive rhetoric that we see that both characterizations are somehow, simultaneously, true, and that despite their exhilarating variety these poems are of a piece and come from one complex, sophisticated, supremely alert sensibility.
　　—Dick Davis, author of *Love in Another Language*
　　　(full text in the foreword on page xi)

FROZEN
CHARLOTTE

POEMS BY
Susan de Sola

ABLE MUSE PRESS

Printed in the United States of America

Library of Congress Control Number: 2019937300

ISBN 978-1-77349-037-3 (paperback)
ISBN 978-1-77349-038-0 (digital)

Cover image: "Lake Superior Frozen Over " by Patrick Moore

Cover & book design by Alexander Pepple

Susan de Sola photo (on page 105) by Isabelle Puts

Able Muse Press is an imprint of *Able Muse*: A Review of Poetry, Prose & Art—at www.ablemuse.com

Able Muse Press
467 Saratoga Avenue #602
San Jose, CA 95129

For Maarten, and Laura, Aran, Alexander, Eve and Benjamin.

. . . though we cannot make our sun
Stand still, yet we will make him run.

—Andrew Marvell

Acknowledgments

I am grateful to the editors of the following journals where many of these poems originally appeared, sometimes in earlier versions:

Able Muse: "Twins"

American Arts Quarterly: "Portrait, Bust"

Ambit: "Frozen Charlotte," "Rotterdam Chiaroscuro," and "*Carnation, Lily, Lily, Rose*"

Amsterdam Quarterly: "Box" and "Jug of Milk"

Birmingham Poetry Review: "Cedar Closet"

Crab Orchard Review: "Buddy"

The Dark Horse: "The Wives of the Poets"

Fringe Magazine: "Old Newsreel," "Nib Nok Nok," and "Two-Part Song"

Frostwriting: "Paola and the Cricket"

The Ghazal Page: "The Wait"

The Hopkins Review: "Cut Out" and "The Up-Rolling of Time"

The Hudson Review: "Camels at the Amsterdam Highway," "Wertheim Park," "Eve Sleeps," and "The Tulips"

KIN Journal: "Miara"

Light: "The Light Gray Suit" and "The Tear"

Lighten Up Online: "Closely Observed Postman"

Measure: "Frozen Charlotte"

Mezzo Cammin: "The Cornell Boxes," "Mouse Time," "Daniel," and "Railroad Bird"

North Dakota Quarterly: "The Wanting Eye"

Per Contra: "Punctuation Gallant"

PN Review: "*Bringing Up Baby*," "What the Woods Know," and "The Matchstick Man"

Raintown Review: "Blind, She Considers Her Lover"

River Styx: "Curse the Moon"

Shot Glass Journal: "ATM" and "The Promise"

Tilt-a-Whirl: "Shrine for 16"

"Blind, She Considers Her Lover" appeared in the anthology *Intimacy*, edited by Debra Kaufman, Richard Krawiec, Stephanie Levin, and Alan Michael Parker (Jacar Press, 2015)

"Frozen Charlotte" appeared in the anthology *The Doll Collection*, edited by Diane Lockward (Terrapin Books, 2016)

"Little Naomi" appeared in *The Great Gatsby Anthology*, edited by Melanie Villines (Silver Birch Press, 2015)

"Twins" appeared in the *Potcake Chapbook: Families and Other Fiascoes*, edited by Robin Helweg-Larson (Sampson Low, 2019)

"The Wives of the Poets" appeared in *The Best American Poetry 2018*, guest-edited by Dana Gioia; David Lehman, series editor (Scribner, 2018)

I thank the Trustees of the Robert Frost Farm in Derry, New Hampshire, and the Hyla Brook Poets for choosing "Buddy" as the winner of the 2018 Frost Farm Prize for Poetry.

I thank all those who read and commented on these poems.

Foreword

Lyric poets—and Susan de Sola is certainly a lyric poet—tend to be most at home in what we might call one dominant mental space, be it longing, or regret, or celebration, or perhaps some more personal nuance of emotion; but whatever it is, one unifying sensibility clearly pervades both the poems' language and their insights. When we begin to read the poems collected here our first impression is one of a tactile, sensuous, often witty delight in surfaces and appearances, of a delighted sensuousness that can glide into rapt sensuality. There is, for example, a wonderfully evocative poem on a vase of tulips and the shapes the tulips make as they wilt and droop; there is a very beautiful love poem that uses the fable of the blind Indians each describing an elephant in a different way (because they have touched different parts of the animal) to anatomize her husband/lover beside her in bed; there are immensely touching (but never mawkishly cute) poems about her children; there are travel poems, and painterly likenesses arising out of chance encounters. Reading through this book, and registering the sheer delight that so many things and people evoke in this poet, I found myself thinking of the seventeenth century poet Thomas Traherne, whose poem "Wonder" begins "How like an angel came I down!/ How bright are all things here!"

But this is by no means our only sense of what is going on here. Beneath the brightness of many poems, beneath their coruscating language and often dazzling technical dexterity, something much deeper and darker often shows through. Then it is not Traherne's rapturous line that seems apposite, but something more like Faulkner's "The past is never dead. It's not even past." In poem after poem what is present is haunted by what is now absent but was once emphatically real and to hand, and very often for this American poet (who now lives in Europe), what is absent is something that happened long ago in Europe but whose resonances seem ineradicable. There is a kind of muddled mute nostalgia in a poem like "At Brighton Beach", with its café run by immigrants from Odessa; a bit of rueful anger and a bit of regret in a poem that describes a photograph of the poet's father with a young nurse in Italy during World War II, and the way her mother had cut the nurse's face from the photograph, but how all this did was to make the absent nurse "prettier yet."

Then there are two poems about Cary Grant that (like many others here) seem to revel in giddy shimmering elegance, but one ends "Grant's father labored as a trouser presser;/ the son in time became a snappy dresser," and the other (about the screwball comedy *Bringing up Baby*), "the whole edifice of skeleton is rubble," with the present glitter ghosted by the past's shadow, by the dead father and his hard-scrabble life, by the unimaginably long dead dinosaur. In both cases what is dead makes the glamour of the present possible, and the poet seems to say we can take our pick as to which state we focus on, but whichever it is, the other is always there too.

Even when it seems that a poem concentrates on something or someone wholly present (as in the many portraits—of lovers, friends, family members, people met because they provide services or sell things), we feel that the life described is placed in a context that seems fated and inescapable because the past has given *this* life, and no other, to this person. Some poems, especially those about the poet's children, celebrate possibility, adventure, the unknown future, but we also sense the speaker's fear for her subjects, for what life can do to individuals, for the way it catches and makes irrevocable, so that from now on one is *this* person only.

Perhaps this is the real secret of why so many of these poems are so haunting; the sense of unspoken, uncontrollable contexts that define and decide a life, and make it immutably what it is. Brooding beneath the often fanciful charm and lighthearted, confident aplomb of the surface of many of Susan de Sola's poems, there is the past and ever-present fact of human loss.

This book has many moods and many messages for any reader who pays the poems collected here the attention they deserve. At times it seems a fairground, at times a graveyard, and neither cancels the other out. It is a mark of Susan de Sola's always persuasive rhetoric that we see that both characterizations are somehow, simultaneously, true, and that despite their exhilarating variety these poems are of a piece and come from one complex, sophisticated, supremely alert sensibility.

—Dick Davis

Contents

viii   Acknowledgments

xi   Foreword

I

5   Bowl of Sea Glass

6   At Brighton Beach

8   Cut Out

9   Buddy

13   The Light Gray Suit, *North by Northwest*

15   Old Newsreel

16   Little Naomi

18   Nib Nok Nok

20   The Wanting Eye

21   Portrait, Bust

II

25   Camels at the Amsterdam Highway

26   Paola and the Cricket

27   Holistic Practice

30   A Party for Kevin

32   Trotsky's Cat

33   Four Frogs

35   Railroad Bird

36   Bluish Animals

37   Mouse Time

III

41   The River Stone

43   Daniel

45   An Agony of Silk

47   The Cornell Boxes

48   Closely Observed Postman

49   Punctuation Gallant

50   The Wait

51   Cedar Closet

53   Rose Gold

54   Box

56   Wertheim Park

58   Miara

IV

61   What the Woods Know

62   Blind, She Considers Her Lover

64   Jug of Milk

66   The Tulips

68   Hollandsche Schouwburg

69   Rotterdam Chiaroscuro

71   The Tear

73   *Carnation, Lily, Lily, Rose*

75   Frozen Charlotte

76   Eve Sleeps

77   In the Dark

V

81   Curse the Moon

82   Shrine for 16

84   Twins

85   The Promise

86   A Bit of Roof

88   ATM

89   The Matchstick Man

90   *Bringing Up Baby*

92   L'Oréal Féria #50

94   The Wives of the Poets

96   The Up-Rolling of Time

98   Two-Part Song

100   Bounty

103   Notes

Frozen Charlotte

I

The years move a washed-out course . . .

Bowl of Sea Glass

Bottles tossed in drunkenness from land
wash to shore as fragments, beveled chips.
The sea batters them, as if a rough sculptor,
and not the conductor of impeccable measures
calcified in urchins' jaws, the crystal
rods of sponges, byssal threads of mussels.
The sea's soft fingers of anemone know
to open in the dark. Parchment worms
glow and ghost-crabs flitter round the shoals.
Pearls form rounds from grit, and razorbacks
cut ovoid troughs. Is all shaped by the sea
to sound its rhythms through precise machines?
No, the sea is a hammer, a rough refiner;
its fistful of pieces from a bottle thrown.
The sea lifts, pounds the glass. Insists on randomness.

At Brighton Beach

New York

Little Russia, Little Odessa, little something?
A busy Sunday on those bustling streets,
where each shop undersells another.
So many shoes, so much plastic leather
sold by brothers in short sleeves,
by babushkas whose ovoid lines,
made for other climes, are poor
at dispersing the summer heat.

I slip into a Georgian place
where grandeur is for sale.
The carpets are a rich maroon,
the true color of carpet, and beneath tinkling
chandeliers, a disco ball for hot Georgian nights
to many of which the walls testify.

Dozens of photos sweat,
the puff-banged, po-faced owner,
his arm around one guest or other,
dares the camera, "shoot me."

The borscht is Georgian,
clear broth and julienne of carrot—
not the color of carpet. "Inedible," I say.
Of the wine, stupidly, I ask, "Is it dry?"
"We have no dry wines in Georgia."
Wine on its way to sugar, but nicely so,
as if, sipping at a Black Sea,
a spoon of sugar is called for.
The piroshki are excellent, a bit sweet, too,
but service is slow.
I reach for my bag,
and walk the streets lightly, sure I know no one.
Assimilation did its dissemination
half a century back—
thick then with familiarity,
borscht-blood thick.

And next to the okay streets
a boardwalk spreads on a city beach.
The ocean yawns back, breathing
that long fraught trip from Russia.
They call it "Little Russia" here,
but the facts are: absolute breach.

Cut Out

My father spent his war in Sicily.
A shy and studious Air Force surgeon,
he cut bodies out of fallen planes
and pieced them together again. Not much fun,
he said, that daily commerce with the dead.
He showed a book of sepia photos one day;
my father and a lady "holding up" Mt. Etna's
smoke. So unlike Dad to mug and play.
Her name was Kate, her curls once fiery red,
faded now to olive brown. A nurse.
He thought that life with her might have been fine.
Her face was snipped from all the shots. Worse,
my mother had cut, hoping he'd forget,
but the years had made her prettier yet.

Buddy

Buddy had loved me long, but from afar.
We never even kissed. His job was cool,
projectionist at the makeshift movie-house
we had in our sandy, summer island village,
collecting reels by wagon dockside, barefoot
like all of us, to play them from the booth.
A self-described "kraut-mick" among the cultured
Upper West Side Jews, he'd smoke some weed
while spools unrolled, his perch a sweetened pot-
head's den, eye level with projector-beam.
July of Fonda's *Julia*; "Jason's" screams,
a rich aroma of weed caught in his beard—
a fun ascent, to see the movies bent.
I never took his thing for me for real.

I think, for Buddy, stoned was steady-state
and being straight became like being high.
He said sharp things that made me laugh and wince.
The finest points of girls I knew he labeled
"bodacious tatas," "tiny hineys" or worse.
He'd lead his blonde-haired collie up the stairs.
(Like all the dogs he'd owned he named her Christy.)
Then high up on the roof we'd sit and talk
and watch the sun spill pink across the bay.

Next spring, hearing that I was newly single,
he surprised me in my dorm, at posh Bryn Mawr.
He'd traveled all that way by motorbike.
He caused a stir. Not knowing what to do,
I took him to the cafeteria,
big Bud absurd with pint of milk and tray,
and slight young preppy fellows gathered round.
One said to me: "I like him. He reminds me
of guys I used to work with, building, summers."
Our small buzz of celebrity. We went
to town *en masse* for pool and dollar beers.
Tall, side-burned Bud in checks and biker leather,
the sum and magnet of our bourgeois dread,
but there was something wholesome to him always.
He slept on my best girlfriend's floor, without
complaint. I realize now he'd hoped for more.
I didn't think about the miles he'd traveled,
his long-held dream deferred, or aim . . . busted.

Then one July he met my wilder sister,
gestured at me and said to her, "I've been
in love with Suze, this woman here, for years"—
and then he bedded her instead. She was
perhaps a bit more than he'd bargained for . . .
"I won't touch that wild cat again," he said.
Next day, he seemed worn-out and quite undone.
In August, he deflowered a friend of mine,
she dying to be unburdened, then ashamed
that it was Buddy—*Buddy!*—who'd been her first.

Then Grandma passed away, and I lost touch—
the place no longer mine. In later years,
I went back once, with husband, kids, and sank
in memory. I saw Bud there in town,
where you see everyone in local bars.
Still bearded, but now trim and clean in linen
shirt and cool white jeans, he looked quite well.
We drank some whiskey sours; he filled me in.
He'd married and was happy, risen to
a Fire Department Captain in the city.
Like many boys, he'd dreamed of fighting fires.
"But me, I guess I never grew up," he grinned.

Some years went by. I heard he'd died, a heedless
mix of medicine and nightly drink.
Died in his chair, still upright, not yet forty.
He'd always liked his substances. He'd claimed
that they "enhanced" his life. What had he needed
in grown-up years after the youthful weed?
A drink or two each night no matter what?
How strange that some small pill had felled my friend,
one strong enough to hoist up hose and ladder,
to carry men through flame, to breathe through smoke.

Chivalric Buddy, unafraid of fire,
yet quenched in liquor, his exit sudden, unplanned.
I recall his kindness, tilted nose, the mystery
that was his face (like many bearded men),
his soft blue eyes, the big and solid frame.
I wonder now, what was his name—his real name?
I wish that I had asked him. I would ask
him now: *Buddy, tell me, what's your name?*

The Light Gray Suit, *North by Northwest*

Everyone wants to be Cary Grant. Even I want to be Cary Grant.
    —Cary Grant

He'd rather walk down Madison, his route
to Oak Bar cocktails, in his perfect suit.

He cuts through tweeds and Technicolor skirts,
a chiseled, dapper gentleman: it hurts

to see him roughed-up, passed out in a cell.
He fares quite badly, but the suit wears well.

Caught bloody-handed with a murderous knife,
he hides aboard a train, meets future wife

Eve, who stows his suit inside her bag
and asks about his monogram. The snag—

the *O* in *R.O.T.* It's meaningless.
He seeks a self, but in unchanging dress.

Dodging a plane, his chances seem so slight.
He's dust-caked. Eve demurs, *Your suit's a fright.*

His being's shaped by some unseen valet;
unlike the jewel-toned Eve, his palette's gray.

A cipher wiped by blanks. A bloodless scene.
He's then locked up; the suit is boxed and clean.

In "off the rack" an active man emerges,
who climbs up steel-framed houses, mountain verges.

Eve's shawl gets torn on trees, she sheds a heel,
but stays kid-gloved and nyloned all the reel.

They cling to giant crowns on Rushmore's mount;
a drab professor ups the body count.

Now Eve in silk paj—CUT!—a scene suppressed!
The tunneled ingress tells us he's undressed.

***

Charisma, granted, carried its own load,
his past submerged beneath the star-paved road.

Grant's father labored as a trouser presser;
the son in time became a snappy dresser.

Oh star of lacquered hair and knife-edged pants,
You too had wished a life like Cary Grant's.

Old Newsreel

Dallas, 1963

The color-slide from blue to teal of skies
and clothes and office signs
tells us they've become less real.
Greens are sorrowful and sage, acid spreads,
the print degrades, bleeding foliage of its age.
Orange tints dilute the reds, no crimson
slash to complement her rusted, pill-boxed,
bee-hived head.

She looks made up, a pancake tan
coats skin ochre, tangerine; we know
that she was elegantly wan.
A wash of charcoal fades the black paint
of cars, dimming duller, glinting gray
on a destined track in a world without
primary color. The years move a washed-out course,
leaching pigments, PCBs, and dolor.

Little Naomi

Baz Luhrmann's The Great Gatsby

He's colorized and caught New York. It's 1922,
when Mommy, my Naomi, was a little toddler-Jew.

I've seen old family photos of her playing in the Park.
The sepia imbues her eyes with dusky, driven dark,

and outside in the snow she sleds, with brother Ithiel,
an angel's name that only Jewish kids could try to spell.

They play, unknowing that the years ahead of them will hold
a crash at home; and over there in Europe will unfold

another war of wars to be unleashed upon their kind.
It wasn't yet on Gatsby's—or on Scott Fitzgerald's—mind;

just the sound of money hovering around his honey,
and my rinky-tink, fur-enrobed, three-year-old Naomi.

Meyer Wolfsheim takes his pay, the bad Wolf of his day,
in a vaguely prescient *Wolf of Wall Street* way.

He's grizzled quite grotesquely; beaky, heavy-browed—a rat.
(Arnold Rothstein, Kingpin Fixer, didn't look like that.)

Naomi is now 94. She seldom leaves her bed;
no Gatsby, no DiCaprio, no East Egg in her head.

But in the corner of the screen, curbside, looking shy,
amid all of the extras, carriage drivers, passersby,

a three-year-old is walking with her daddy hand in hand.
There's the muff and there's the cap. And here's our newfound land.

Nib Nok Nok

Nib nok nok
hreft and cleft,
pick axet splitd
sholid, sit
the pressd, presst,
shist, shale,
so chunk, hunkd
only thickt
braze brickt
brazz, schrape,
so stillt and stilt,
glitz staint,
vein o kilk
wint bround
shoft fround,
shiver over
klichen klover,
nok nok
I ema a. . . .

translation:

Knock knock, who's there?
with heft and cleft
pick axe split
solid, sit
the press, press
of schist and shale,
so chunk, hunk,
only thick
brazen brick,
raze, scrape,
still and sit,
glitz stains,
calcium veins
wind around
soft ground,
slivers over
lichen, clover,
knock, knock . . .
I remain a rock.

The Wanting Eye

We walked the craters of Mt. Etna,
our pockets full of broken lava;
the ancient molten flow made slow
until it stopped in time as stone.
We walked the pebbled, cindered rims.
My daughter danced upon the scrim
of Typhon, she could feel the fire
not yet put out; we scrabbled higher
to see the colors that are born
when petrified: the umber, ochre,
terra, pink, but largely darkest,
rubbled black. I took the hardest,
blackest stone, of cold compact.
I felt its chill. I put it back.

Portrait, Bust

I layer clay and hope he'll coalesce,
begin to plane his jaw and hone his cheek,
his heavy brow, his nose's prow. Distress.
His ear is wrong, I slice it off. I see
a flaw, pry out his eye, the whole not right.
Relief to stroke his cheek or flatten down
odd locks of hair, but still not him. Too slight,
and mean. It seems he now returns my frown.
A man, and yet not mine, this portrait bust.
He stares out coolly from Swiss mountain mud.
I see just why it's failed, and fail it must,
this blend of burial earth and stony blood.
I love the living head, the breathing face.
I fear the sculpture that would take his place.

II

As if it knows we are to blame . . .

Camels at the Amsterdam Highway

Bactrians under the overpass
cut the view with double humps,
like mini-dunes or mountaintops
that cross the flats and slate-blue sky.

Watered here in daily rain,
far from desert sun and sage,
salt pans, dunes and heat-borne flies,
needlegrass and Gobi shrubs,

they rest on knees and arch their necks,
oblivious to highway trucks
that hurtle down the overpass.
They deign to graze the plain Dutch grass.

Paola and the Cricket

He'd wanted a frog, not a tarantula or snake.
It seemed simple: a dish for rocks, water and plants,
and a daily diet of live crickets. She'd buy whole batches,
crawling. She teased them out one by one with pincers.
Squat and still, the tongue, uncoiled, cleft
and sticky would ladle one in, the great jaws
of hell swinging shut, in bug-eyed glaze of fixity, and muscular chewing.
Hating it, she kept up the system; her son expected it.
One rogue bug escaped, disdained his fate as frog food,
fish food or fish bait. Found a way under the floorboards,
to the crawl spaces, a warm duct or molding panel,
lived there on soggy bits, smaller bugs, or spores.
In the perpetual dark, he sawed wings, their serrated edges
and acoustical sails to bloom each night, marring her sleep.
For months he sang with his wings—
to wail his brothers' fates? To lure a mate? To castigate?
Three months she did not sleep, a thousand auguries,
and at crack of dawn, they met again, bleary-eyed
in the bathroom light. He was fat and silent, he'd prospered below.
It took not a moment's thought. She shot her wool-slippered foot
from the flaps of her robe. Crushed it on the spot.

Holistic Practice

She's late, pink-flushed, and flaked with drift,
she brings a draft, a blast of wind.
Though she forgot to bring a gift,
she gives her wishes, many more!
Her red scarf drags across the floor.

Across from me, she picks a dish,
hand-cut fries with battered fish.
The fries are hard, the fish no catch:
"*The bottom of the pot*," she says.
Would they fry up a fresh new batch?

The salt and mayo crust her lip.
She's got a one-room flat in town,
so cheap she fears to let it slip.
Those years ago, Arts funds were flush;
she danced, performed, explored—no rush.

Fifty, a therapist today—
"Holistic Practice" shows the way
to speak and walk and think and be,
through guided movement, voice and breath.
"*Holism's the holistic key.*"

The brain's made "wide" beneath her touch,
the organs revved, the bones aligned,
secretions flow. Who knew how much
one might acquire? An untold wealth
of harmony, of life itself!

Who knew it was so hard to live—
and of this wisdom she could give?
That mostly we do nothing right:
not sit, draw breath, lie down, or speak—
our backs too loose, our chests too tight.

She's certified, trains teachers in
imparting equilibrium.
Alone, she mostly dwells within.
She's finished with her history.
Her query's brief, perfunctory:

"*The kids?*" She knows I am a mother.
Uneasy that my life is other,
I pass on quickly, knowing that
in seconds more she'll offer me
prized photos of her aging cat.

It seemed to me that cats are good
at the holistic way of life:
in balance—Zen—and that they would
exemplify all that we might
attain if she could teach us right.

But no, her Boop, he was her treasure;
her angel and her source of pleasure.
"Oh, look, how cute!"—a cat bow tie!
I grin and nod, divided by
a deep, holistic urge to cry.

A Party for Kevin

This bash for a piglet is really to show off
Philippe's stylish new home, a forge renovation
reclaimed for the gentry, and Kevin
is the perfect gentleman's perfect accessory.
The round of his snout softly kisses the ground;
he seems to have hair, blond bristles, lashes that fringe
a frosty and appraising blue eye.
He trots by on trotters, an ambulant meal, his round forms
roulades and cold cuts
ready for carving with steel knives.
Only a piglet, he blithely ignores us,
snuffles among tables and finely shod feet,
wagging his tiny vestigial tail.
In his sharp quest for fallen food,
he may fool us into thinking
he's some sort of dog.
It's hard not to scoop Kevin up like a baby,
but in one brash wriggle he wrestles free,
goes on with his search, hovering near the buffet—
where *we* are offered shashlik.
We sense the slippage and make *pork* of pig.
"Lamb," I'm assured. "Or beef," but I taste it as pork.
Could Kevin smell it, this breach of manners?
It drives him to drink: he laps
a forgotten gin-tonic with sparklers
someone left on the floor.
I run to retrieve it, feeling slightly absurd,

the strangest good deed—that
and the towel I'd ordered for him embroidered with *Kevin*.
It rests now on the banquette heaped with gifts:
a blanket, a beach ball, (four) winter mittens,
a leash, water dish, a wading pool,
a collar with *Kevin* spelled out in zirconias,
a mud pack, a brush.
Kevin, Kevin—a Pig Complete.

Months later, I stopped by to see him.
He'd grown large and imposing,
his peeps now an ear-splitting screech.
He'd trampled the roses,
chewed up the kilims, and broken a chair.
Philippe found that, when engaged on the phone,
tossing an apple kept Kevin busy crunching.
Going Pavlov one better, clever Kevin
connected the dots and exploded in wails,
demanding an apple as soon as it rang.
Unhappy, left too much alone, likely staring,
impatient, at the silent telephone. By year's end,
he'd been moved to a petting farm, content
among bunnies and lambs and squat ducks.
Yet still, he ignores us—no need to impress—
though when children pat Kevin, he seems to allow it.
Perhaps they remind him of when he was little,
a prince among piglets, and seemed to us to have it all.

Trotsky's Cat

Büyükada

for Nor

Walking the roads of Princes' Island, place of exile
and waiting, we pick our steps,
watchful for broken stones worn by centuries
into unfamiliar patterns.

I see it approaching, a dirty calico
of no particular beauty, a cat dingy with Ottoman dust.
It crouches low while moving forward, eyes fixed
on an impromptu gathering of sparrows,
all hops and cocks, oblivious.

It moves as low as fast, textile belly
one with the paving, to promise the improbable,
that spring could overtake wing,
the small neck of the bird shaped to fit
the space between slender canines.

But then the carriage comes, eight hooves pounding,
wheels squealing, a peal of bells—
a warning snapped up by the birds, lifted.

The calico frozen, one paw still raised
to compensate the spectacle with a frieze.
Its glance is bleak, cast over us quickly,
as if it knows we are to blame.

Four Frogs

Four frogs had fallen through the grate
into the basement window box,
amid some soil, a moss-grown ball,
a bag, a Bic in shocking pink.

We slipped a plank in for escape—
no use. They sat as still as stones,
squared off. A friend with grit and defter
fingers dared to scoop them out.
We dumped the box into our yard.

Two large, one weak, one small; each leapt
away, opposed, alone, at speed.
The weeks behind that glass had bred
no love, but why take leave with such
alacrity—such vehemence?
I asked three nearest dear to me:

Eve:

Just hate. Cellmates in contest for
the scarce bug, branch, or drop of rain.
They'd stare and breathe and breathe and stare.
The other frogs were all the world,
a *summum* bleak, unbearable.
They could not even see the sky.
Pure rivals. *Hell is other frogs.*

Benjamin:

Indifference. They failed to see
or register their fellow frogs,
who may as well have been just stones.
Those stares were empty. Weakened still,
their sheer immovability
conferred invisibility.
Confined, the stop in time and place
imposed on each a kind of sleep.
On each a sweeping solitude.

Alexander:

It's simple, neither hate nor choice,
or even mere indifference.
They're only frogs for heaven's sake!
They parted to improve their odds,
to find fresh food, to hide once more.
Escape is all about one's turf.
Commandment without sentiment:
The frog hunts best who hunts alone.

Or has my memory transformed
what they said to what I heard
as their own thoughts? *The kids I knew
leapt like frogs their separate ways.*

Railroad Bird

Little railroad bird,
I give you a bite:
a flake of croissant
sets your feathers in flight.
No fear of the shod,
you take butter, batter.
Your head seems to nod,
little bird on the tracks,
cementing a deal.
You're as tall as my ankles,
that small, that real.

Bluish Animals

In answer to Louise Bogan and Henry David Thoreau

Bluish monkeys, one small shrew,
the cat they call the Russian blue,
the purebred rat, and peacocks, too—

yes, bluish on the land are few.
But bluebird is defined by blue,
and countless sorts that fly or flew.

The largest animal's the whale,
his head is blue, and so's his tail.
So many fish are blue of scale!

Being confined to air or sea,
these challenge visibility,
as though for God especially,

for camouflage may make us blind;
to earthly elements confined,
while blue is heaven's private mind—

for sea and sky have no real hue,
it's light they borrow shining through.
Although they may be hard to view,
a wealth of animals are blue.

Mouse Time

They say all creatures' hearts may last
an equal number of beats,
a billion for the whale as for the mouse,
an equal measure to be drawn.

And so the whale's slumbrous drum
for decades dilates water rings,
and so the mouse, from dawn to dawn
spins whole seasons on a wheel.

The scrap of mammal sings
a rushed song of hurrying mouse,
the too-long tail marks its trail—staccato zeal,
a countdown of time—in starts.

III

There is cruelty in the boxes . . .

The River Stone

I think of how you helped to lug
that big green river stone, and filled
your coat with smaller ones for me.
A soft jade-green, and shot with white
inclusions, cumbering that Tyrol
riverbed downstream, it beckoned
with green and softness; how it seemed
at once to glint and weep, but was
a trick of water in the light.

The stones were heavy, hard to hold.
I slid the big one, like a great
bear's paw or flattened heart, beneath
the front car seat. We carried it
a thousand miles of highway home.
Our only walk together, most days
you skied. I wandered off alone,
my steps a metronome of tears
that fell on fresh-bared earth, and pocked
the scabs of gray indifferent snow.

The year of tears. I cried a year.
Always alone; in buses, bed,
at night, at love. And no one saw.
I wonder now if I ran out.
The stone is here, gone gray. No place
to put it now. It presses down
on books, with only one side seen.
Complete fool's errand. In a bowl,
the small ones rest in drier comfort,
no longer scattered shining on
that riverbed, below dark peaks,
whose endless, flowing rivulets
had held me there, and had me fooled.

Daniel

"I would have made a good mother," she said,
a quiet conviction. "We visit once a year,
we gave him a grave . . . Daniel."

Is it a name if he never knew it was his?
Perhaps he heard it, in those first hours,
which were also the last hours.

Small and slow-blinking, eyes bewildering
blue, with slips of fingers
that would not curl,

he could hear her, and knew
her voice from before.
"Daniel," she must have said, many times.

"The hardest part was giving him back,
but the nurse was kind."
"Daniel," she must have said,

many times, in all scales, making
a name. During those few hours,
too long and too short, it was mostly a word

among other words. But still, it carried love,
called to a person, and while not unique—
think of all the Daniels—

it made individual. The love in its sounds
conferred the person. It was spoken,
before it was engraved.

An Agony of Silk

Her voice, it seemed, had licked a thousand ashtrays,
spat out a thousand butts. She was big-busted
and tall, with bleach-dead hair—no longer young.
This was her lair, a small select boutique
of silken panties, bras with bows and lace.
It was as if she lived inside a closet,
one owned by some confined, imagined being
whose life was lived entirely on a bed,
supine, in wait, yet neither dressed nor naked.

I asked about a famous brand, and if
she carried any clothing from them, too.
Afraid I don't. It's too expensive, tight!
The girls who have the body can't afford
them yet, and those who have the money, well
those gals . . . they no longer have the body.

Her vision was a bleak trajectory,
tragic and pitiless, of older women
broadening in the beam, where bulges push
against the pleats and strain the seams; a waste
of worsted, airy lace disgraced and stretched,
an agony of angel skin in tints of silk.

Now she adjusts herself to face her clients,
and, elbows propped on till, her chin in hand,
she calculates, dispensing her advice.
She catwalks to some drawers discreetly closed,
takes out the seldom seen: foundation garments,
the stuff that lies—caressing, next to skin,
the only thing that touches some of us.

What journey brought her to this countertop?
She understands the women here in town,
where life is fat. She knows the curves and swells
that years accrue and those it takes away.
How *hot* she must have been ten years ago!

Does what she earns enable her to buy?
And yet she has (and doesn't have) the goods,
but by some lucky odds, the body still.
Ensconced here, day by day, she sees what is.
She wraps the neat, consolatory boxes
and ties them up with silken, black lace bows,
for those who, never naked, dress to undress.

The Cornell Boxes

There is cruelty in the boxes.
Cornell, boxed in, dreaming the box,
the box-office dreams of beautiful women,
fine ballerinas, Medici jewels, and whole planets,
a fine balance of thin bits of paper, sturdy planks and nails,
Joseph and his hammer and plane, shavings and planks and panes
of glass. A carpenter of glass, an architect of stasis. Not one more minute
will come to pass, as all is boxed in, with one side reserved for glass, there is only
one way to look in, one view. They always face from the stage, like the old idea of the ballet
that one must never turn one's back to the king, and a profile position might be a dangerous thing.
The feet splay sideways, and that crab dance hops its submission. So look through that glass,
but never touch a thing. And this is the great ambition of it, at its most naked, because
assemblage trumps imitation, which is only made of paint or clay. A Cornell box
is loot stolen from random scavenges, feverish clippings, flat taxonomies of
birds and beings, a dedication to drowning silence. The roar and fury
of that box! It's terrifying. To open it courts peril, you unleash—
or it just crumbles into drab vintage dyes, Lucite cubes,
shrinking paper and planets that roll like marbles.
This is the art of it, its inviolability, a promise
we stand before, conspire to keep,
as Joseph kept it, alone.

Closely Observed Postman

for JB

I see rubber dangle
from the branch of a tree.
I suspect that our postman
leaves bands here for free.

His mailbag starts full
of postcards and letters,
and flyers new-sprung
from red rubber fetters.

He needs no small trophies
when finished, no scraps
to mark emptied perfection
and celebrate laps.

So he leaves them behind,
but not scattered or thrown.
He hangs them on branches
as though they had grown.

Each round, openmouthed,
elasticized sphere
speaks for the postman:
Look well, I was here.

Punctuation Gallant

Guillemets was going to Interpunct his Solidus
with a Bullet, or possibly a Dagger or Caret,
making Hash of his Numero, just two Degrees north
of his Ditto mark. He narrowly missed the Octothorpe,
dislodging his Obelus (always an Ordinal Indicator
of a man in his Prime). But Pilcrow Tilde the Section sign,
Underscoring his Understrike with a Broken Bar or Pipe.

It was the Currency of Asterism with a Tee;
Uptack and Indexed Fist, his Lozenge of Irony
and a Tie to his Diacritical Remarks about Non-English
Brackets for all but his Whitespace characters.
All of his Inverted Exclamations were to Nought.
He went out Backslash, with Dash and a great Interrobang.

The Wait

Camellias brown: they've just survived their winter burn.
I cut back damaged branches. The blooms curl close, they wait.

I pace the garden while you wander free. It darkens;
the wall of brick grows blood-red dim as shadows wait.

Alone, I sculpt the bed, a solitary curve,
trace your form in lounges, in planes that will not wait.

This earth conceals the cables that bind us as we talk,
and signals fill the cloud, forever made to wait

for hearts that must be watered, agitations pruned.
Our garden runs to riot as I weed and wait.

I've scraped the stones and gathered up the leaves. How long,
how long do you expect me to keep still and wait?

I scratch a sign across the bricks, a ragged nail
and scuffed-up boot, just tapping out the time I wait.

Small piles of burning leaves send smoke up to the sky.
A lily swells with sun and seed. In stillness, she must wait.

Cedar Closet

She's hung the suits of meaty tweed and twill,
aridified furs and heavy shearling coats,
and set in boxes scarves and gartered stockings.
Plummy satins with acrylic buttons
carved into flowers, her widow's wedding suit
in watered lavender. She's kept the first,
seed-pearled wedding gown concealed.

Repelled by a stole of baby foxes, mouth to tail
to claw-like clasp, I stroke the velvet hats
with veils and pins, and sueded platform pumps.
I try her rhinestone-studded party shoes,
and lift her slips in tints of angelskin,
her stacks of gloves in suede and calf and kid,
her handkerchiefs, initialed N.L.P.,
obsolete these seventy years.
                                        He'd climbed
a mine-sown hill to save a soldier. A trap.
Blown up, he set off more while rolling down.
There wasn't very much of him left.
                                        She's kept
for me the graduated pearls, too small
for my taste, and a dress of painted silk
that somehow fits, as does the pleated skirt
and ochre Pringle sweater set.
                                        Forgotten,
the tarnished powder compacts, random lipsticks
and yellowed hankies slipped in every clutch,

in leather bags with heavy metal clasps
that snap shut—tight like the purse of her lips,
her clothes the only story that she tells.
A puff of dust drifts down the cedar walls.

Rose Gold

Some rose gold lost in autumn gold—
in piles of beech and maple leaves—
a hoop of gold lies in the mold.
A promise gone, a woman grieves

at how the green remembered spring
is lost in dark and wet compost.
Yet when the snows have claimed the ring,
it is the leaves I'll miss the most.

Box

He went
and left
behind
his things
where lies
a box
to bring
outside
the things
he left
behind
he left
no box
to bring
his things
outside
the things
are here
but he
is not
this is
the box
that time
begot—
how can
it be
that mold

can mean
the form
of man
and yet
its rot?

Wertheim Park

Amsterdam

The woman rubbed her hands and stamped her feet.
We were gathered in winter in the Wertheim Park.
You forgot your gloves, I said in sympathy.
She gestured to her purse, and muttered *work*.

We'd come for the annual memorial march.
She stood in the shelter of an oak, her back to the stage,
apart from the crowds that filled the level park.
I wondered as I saw a man about her age

facing her, rocking heels, misting breath,
his quite large ears rimmed pink with cold.
Her hands began to move. I saw he was deaf.
She signed the things the mayor and the rabbi said.

Like frozen birds, her hands rose up and fell,
her black brows frowned and her face seemed to dance.
Her mouth made O's, as if too shocked to tell;
words flew through her eyes and fluttering hands.

I watched him watching her in mute oration.
His hands in pockets, his mind tracks in silence
back sixty-seven years, to liberation,
the buried history of his lost parents.

The rabbi's prayers began: to remember them,
and all the numberless, nameless dead,
and all the known, too many to name,
so he sang a litany of camps instead.

Interlaced in the Hebrew melody:
Auschwitz, Belzec and *Theresienstadt,*
Westerbork, Dachau, Drancy, Treblinka.
How did she sign those names? What signs for that?

All I recall is her mouth made an O,
her hard brows as the general hell repeated,
all the names the same: O, O, O, and O.
Auschwitz, Belzec, and *Theresienstadt,*

Westerbork, Drancy, Treblinka, Dachau,
a crescendo of unspecified despair.
Could she speak the names with signs? Then how?
Still, her tireless hands cut the frozen air.

Miara

The Jewish Cemetery, Marrakesh

In this graveyard in Morocco
old tombs are incognito;

flattened slabs of stone
abrade and bleach to bone—

no letters, sculpture, form
defy the earth and worm.

Pale dogs nose around
to guard the sacred ground.

I found more recent stones,
a place for fresher bones?

It seemed here, from the piles
of rocks, red flower styles

and scattered petals, new death
had come, but the boy's last breath

was lost to cholera long ago.
Who nursed that ancient sorrow?

Only ten, he had no heir,
yet summoned fifty years of care.

I asked, was this not also to exist?
Marbled, tended, mothered—missed.

IV

In stillness she must wait . . .

What the Woods Know

I call up my lover in the woods—
would he were here—and I tell
him about leaf-gold and everything bare
bearing him, borne away, and no sounds

but dogs' barks and bark sloughs
and bites of wind and a bitter
yellow fungus that looks unreal
and mushroomed troughs.

Trouw in Dutch means *marriage* and *true*.
It would be all those things,
cradled in a phone, cradled in an ear,
if he were not there, if he could be here.

Hearing him, I make a small turn in the gloaming,
heel resolute, the hang-up click.
But here he still is, in a shadow of birds
flying, slowly homing.

Blind, She Considers Her Lover

Six blind Indians felt the elephant
and made of it six entities.
So is my love, for in the dark,
where half a marriage is spent,
you are many.

First there is that silky fringe
of frontward falling hair—
you are a horse, fetchingly groomed.
You shake your head and your forelock falls
forward, steed.

Then there are your collarbones which roll,
like the bone of shells rolled by water
collected in pebbles and driftwood and weed—
you are shells on a beach,
resting in kelp-hollows.

Then the smooth skin of your back
and chest, it sings with softness.
You are bolts and drapes of some rich fabric,
organic weave of silk to velvet—
yes, you are a draper's treasure.

Lower, there is warmth, and coils, springs;
countless corkscrews of millimeter breadth.
I would guess a fine steel wool,
its gauge innumerable zeros.

The legs are sturdy, lightly forested,
surely they are lichened logs.

Yet between the moss and the steel,
the strangest skin, unlike any other,
stretched, nerve-rich, another color.
Even if I were a blind Indian I'd know it;
it is itself, it is not like another.

Jug of Milk

Vermeer's The Milkmaid

She caresses the jug,
the milk tops the table.
A foursquare hand,

its robust thumb
sidles up the handle
as though in soft connection

through the green cloth of a magician's table,
through a rough stone floor
to earth and worms and grass and cows.

We are born and go
from milk to meat
to earth to worms

to grass to feed a cow again
(and the Dutch know cows).
But here, in this Vermeer,

the light, which is none of these things,
makes a great deal good.
The earthy Dutch, they caught that light,

pounded it in pigments (earth again),
but still, it seeps out;
a wondrous milky haze

here in the museum
enfolds my shoulders,
lets me forget those cows,

lets me think everything is light.

The Tulips

We bought them at a farmer's field, so plump
and red—great goblets, plush concavities
which made of content an irrelevancy.
For days we took delight in their postmortem
magic. What had this red exuberance
to do with death? They anchored down the table,
held center stage, just like an aria,
a swelling note we held against the odds.

But now they start to fall apart, and see,
they deconstruct so cleanly! Diving petals
reveal a pattern on the inner corner,
a three-point wedge of aubergine black, capped
by arching yellow bands—a stylized print
of itself in little—vector to the ribbed red
flank, which had barely aged. The tiny tulip-
print anticipates its slide to symbol.
The sleekly flattened violet pistils spill
out scarcely any powder. Slim green stalks
with small white crowns stand bare. Abstract.
A Dutch-bobbed slouching flapper of a flower,
so modernist and sleek, a silhouette.
A flower a cartoonist might invent.

I sweep the petals up in great big bunches,
the dustbin blazing; it had never looked better.
But it's become almost a game. The petals
fall at random—yet they seem to fall
in answer to our conversation, plunging
at key words, thumping downward during our
significant pauses, heard in silences.
Blowsy, lipsticked interlocutors;
drunken smacks, and dried-out goodbye kisses.

Hollandsche Schouwburg

We walked in silence to the Wall of Names;
I peered at the letters and it seemed quite mad—
de Sola and *Pool*—the spelling just the same—
the names for cousins that I might have had.

Some thankful American dispensation,
one branch that serendipity would spare,
the trick of a forefather's emigration,
it seemed a shameful miracle that I stood there.

Rotterdam Chiaroscuro

The sun shines more on some than others,
And so we envy our French brothers . . .

Too much wine in the afternoon,
they are selling French Provençal scenes
to sun-starved Dutchmen
and the flowers in lavender are copious in the giant urn.

Smooth, white pants and suede heels on the flagstones,
and sparkling flutes served from a tray
made to look like a palette, by a third daughter
in a rented white waiter's tenue.

Les Arlésiennes are dappled,
and thin white garden chairs tilt
in shadows that make manifest the sun,
the sun that shoots through *Les citrons*,
drowns in the murky center of *Le demitasse*,
rebounds from the keel line of *Le bateau bleu*.

Sidling past views of *La plage* and the
Baie de Marseilles, we loosen our June wool jackets,
on for the chill, and wonder about the heavy fog
of smells from the cheese banquet, whole rounds
driven over from Calais, laid open with butter knives,
dank with bacteria in their crusts and veins.

We know the artist is a French doctor, prolific
in *le week-end*, and the dealers flush from a thriving business
in bedpans, crab-foot canes, and walkers.

It was art for art's own sake, and yes, *Coquelicots*
would match the couch, and so the cash was laid down
for the sun, and for the shadows.

The Tear

The local sage of lingerie,
I passed her shop again today.
I need to ask her for advice,
I've torn a hole in costly tights.
It's quite discreet—behind the knee—
so, will it hold? If none can see,
is it worthwhile to replace?
Well, though it's small, it's a disgrace.
My dear, don't wear a garment—ever—
that has a flaw. Oh never, never!
I listened to this aging girl
in hopes of yet another pearl.
For just imagine you were in
an accident, what deep chagrin
you'd feel to have your holey tights
revealed beneath the theatre lights
in hospital. You'd be exposed!
But, by what reasons I supposed
would one believe that flaws inside
one's undergarments override
broken bones and loss of breath,
concussion, burns, or risk of death?

Perhaps there's no protection from
fatality? If it's to come,
let one's tenue remain exact,
preserve one's dignity intact.

This is one's armor, she would say,
it keeps old Chaos far away.
Do right by it—*There's nothing sadder*
than a nylon with a ladder,
a clasp unclasped or stay unstayed.
Join in the fray, but stay unfrayed.
If life somehow gives you the slip,
at least you've not displayed the rip.
Buy but beware. Be groomed. Take care.
Enfin, you are your underwear.

Carnation, Lily, Lily, Rose

John Singer Sargent

What had they caught? As if those Japanese lanterns glowing
pink and teal were full of fireflies or glow worms.

The girls' black boots and stockings tread on the uncut grasses
and wildflowers and fortuitous lilies.

They stir with sticks, as if whirling fireflies to generate light,
a small buzz of protest ricochets against the paper prison.

Just two girls amid the profusion of fires and flowers,
their four feet, four hands, in white butterfly casings.

A girl myself, I stared long at this painting, trying to gather
its meaning, the mystery of its technology, the alluring toy they had.

Now, if a Sargent, I'd prefer a *grande dame*, monumental, frontal,
but here are his ladies in the making, making the light

lighting up their faces, heads tilted down, absorbed, not yet inclined
to let their faces take on the painter's paint.

And very far away, on a Japanese bay, a thousand lanterns rattle,
the celebration unknown in England, where girls toy with souvenirs

hoping to coax fire from paper, heedless of lilies and carnations,
while their black boots stamp down the garden grasses and blooms,

and the white arms of the girls clasp whole globes, spinning out the light.

Frozen Charlotte

I am a doll of ivory bisque.
I was a girl, but was too bold.
To preen in silks, I dared to risk
the open sleigh. I don't grow old.
A girl of flesh who died of cold.

I froze while riding to the ball,
to end in ice and snowy pearls.
I thawed in kilns, a molded doll,
a pocket vanitas for girls.
My cheeks are flushed. I died of cold.

I float now in a child's bath.
My little mistress pushes me
from rim to rim or to her mouth.
They've taken all my finery.
A doll's not flesh. I don't get cold.

I'm safe for play—no moving parts.
My price is small. I'm bought and sold.
I fortify their frozen hearts.
I'm getting warmer now—it's told
on mountain roads. I died of cold.

Eve Sleeps

Each night we form a double C.
Hand rests on hip or curves to breast,
chest to back, his strong legs pressed
to make a chair of flesh for me.
Adjudications of the breath,
Adam's apple near my head,
we're stacked for storage in this bed
as sleep suspends us near a death.
Twins in the dark, we knit a seam
from toe to crown, a tensile wire.
Our eyes roll blind, they roll desire.
Locked in body, branched to dream,
we fall into this darker space.
Each cannot see the other's face.

In the Dark

At extremely low light-levels
the signal may be entirely drowned out
by the noise,
and even a top-of-the-range camera
won't focus
on a featureless surface.

When you look at, for example,
a sheet of white paper,
your mind adjusts
so that it matches the white to what
you are expecting to see.

Your camera, however, has no
expectations. The color it sees
is the actual color present.

But we perceive as neutral
the various shades of white
that light up a scene, a trick
our brains perform
to maintain a sense of normality.

All the devices round us generate noise—
the background hiss of a radio,
the subterranean siss
of an amped-up electric guitar,
the interference of a badly tuned TV.

At extremely low light-levels,
the signal may be drowned out
entirely by the noise, the silent noise
that roars, granular and gray.

V

A forest fire of one . . .

Curse the Moon

When my son learned at four, to give the finger, he didn't dare
Give it me, or you or sundry. But one night, looking out his window
Saw a scrap of moon, and annoyed by its perpetual if now enervated stare,
Thrust the full two inches of his middle digit to the cosmos,

And his shock the next evening when the moon didn't show,
Convinced he'd insulted it, never doubting his power,
His apologies profuse, muttered aloud, his tones low.
He'd thought it gone for good—relieved when it returned, decorous,
                              If reversed—at the appointed hour.

Shrine for 16

For he considers the top of his bureau.

For he has been given a damp rag, and urged to create order.

For he has bottles of Armani and Axe, and centers each on a Heineken beer mat.

For he has folded two pairs of sunglasses—cheap and never worn—but kept.

For he has made a diagonal display of three oversized watches—manly, fake, and much wanted (yet his phone has displaced them).

For he has dusted three ashtrays and four lighters.

For he has scattered a profusion of pot pipes, three with ornamental stamp *City of Amsterdam.*

For he has a frosted shot glass printed with cannabis leaf.

For he has two cool Buddhas to keep watch, the fat and laughing kind.

For he has made his centerpiece a bottle of Bacardi Razz (proof he'll be 18), its seal unbroken.

For it is flanked with two cocktail glasses from a disco, in yellow and blue, bearing stamped images of surfboards.

For he has kept my cut-up Amex card; it, too, is cool.

For he has two boxes of condoms (still in their cellophane), in tangerine and teal.

For he has kept two well-creased Durex singles still in their foil, often rubbed in contemplation between finger and thumb.

For a big bong squats left, a Balmoral cigar case rising improbably from its funnel.

For he has a bottle opener decorated with a scorpion.

For he has a pencil sharpener shaped like a deck of playing cards.

For his key ring bears the ancient profile of the Playboy bunny.

For he has kept a Jägermeister mini from our hotel bar.

For he has a laser in the form of a tiny pistol, that once caused a flap at airport security.

For he has hung above these things a fallen street sign, whose arrow now points northwest.

For he has impaled a beer mat on the nail that hangs it.

For on the nail dangles a bottle opener, an ergonomically shaped female torso in tin.

For it is ready for the grasp of his puppyish, oversized hand.

For he has set on the lip of the bong a plastic doll: a yellow, white-gloved, grinning M&Ms man.

For he waxes manly and grows boyish.

For he grows.

Twins

A stolen morning, long in bed.
I hold you near my cradled head,
entangled in our common doze,
our hands in hands, and toes on toes.
We'd told the kids we'd sleep in late,
but heard a knock; one could not wait.
We were not up, as rules require,
subordinating our desire
to duties that inhere in mother.
This first sortie without her brother,
feet like small buds peep under flannel;
her head just clears the bed-board panel.
A tiny finger to her lip,
she gazes, haltingly lets slip,
that she is thinking, taking measure
of our strange rarity of leisure,
of our appearing one, though two.
While barely speaking yet, she knew
that it was somehow less, and other
than her deep bond with her twin brother.
What play of judgment at this vision
directs her gesture's slow precision?
The finger rises up and limns
us, then the word that ends begins
its verdict: *Twins . . . you . . . are . . . not . . . twins.*

The Promise

We'll sail a small boat on the lake,
and I will steer so you may sit.
When fifty years trail in our wake,
we'll sail a small boat on the lake.
The wave of time about to break
shall fill the vessel we two fit.
We'll sail a small boat on the lake,
and I will steer, so you may sit.

A Bit of Roof

black shaft, webbed:
dry, it is prone,
flapping limply

erect, it points,
marks, at stepped
intervals, a third leg

wet, a full-reverse
flower domed
with aspiration,

an empty cup
downturned
to reroute

not gather,
a hardwood
flower, a stamen

dry and carved,
hand-handled
its root up,

it moves
perambulates,
adumbrates

a shadow
without sun
suitable,

bespoke,
it gives
temporary shelter

temporarily,
we are snails, armadillos,
and turtles.

ATM

Somehow, it's sexual,
the rim crotch-high,
the shuffling buttocks,
the hands fumbling in secret.

Gone the dainty dialogue,
the date stamp in a little leathery
book of records, at set times. Now,
an onanism of cash, walls with mouths.

The Matchstick Man

takes great leaps
on his one pale leg.
Bounds with relish,
saltates with snap,

florid, russet-haired,
bulbed like a baster,
slubbed with sulfur.

He smiles dithyrambs,
ardent as a dog,
ecstatic to see me.

Suddenly, he leaps,
spins to a headstand,
grovels along the emery—

a long, intense
nuzzle of the head
until it flicks into flame.

His browning glory
a forest fire of one—
one with our rough places.

Bringing Up Baby

1938, Katharine Hepburn and Cary Grant

for CW

Life is like that, running round a swamp
in search of a jaguar, or the crucial bone.
The jaguar's on the loose: it doesn't belong here.
See how it's doubled to its dangerous
and deadly carny brother, unrepentant
and marked out for destruction. Will they find
their pet, or get a fatal bite by moonlight?
See how, in the end, the jaguars usher us
to jail, for safety; trapped in vaudeville.

Life is like that: loons may be mistaken
for jaguars, and big-game hunters miss their targets,
where men are prey, and Cary's—David's—frigid
fiancée, Miss Swallow, will not swallow.
Miss Hepburn's Susan refuses her obvious,
inborn lot. She'll smack those cocktail olives,
lift a car, and mock a moll, but still—
May Robson, dowager queen, so large with wealth,
steals every scene, so certain of her right.

A dog may bark to distraction, and bit by bit
undig a store of stolen boots, while Cary's
dressed in feathered robes or hunting gear,
his options clear. All seems to depend on finding
that intercostal clavicle, the *clou*,
of the dinosaur he'd reassemble.
And yet, from ruined suits to broken glass
to shattered geese, there's nothing Auntie's
pot of gold—the magic grant—can't fix.

But Cary's still fixated on that dog,
he's trailing him *like Hamlet's ghost*, says Robson,
as if the simple link, the simple story
is only dog to bone, and how to fit
a dinosaur's old bones into their places.

Life is like that—Hepburn's swathe of chaos,
the heated hunt, and sliding into water
up to one's chin, by treacherous roots and moonlight.
They fall, and, rolling, smash up Cary's glasses.
It brings him close to her, if only to let
her see the true dark beauty of his eyes.
Kate will sway with delight until the whole
edifice of skeleton is rubble.

L'Oréal Féria #50

Medium Brown

for MM

Aristotle said the middle way is golden;
   but better said, it is to be brunette—
      to average out the black and blonde, to soar with middle flight:
         Meden Agan, the Delphic wisdom, Socratic mean,

the Middle State, the Middle Way, Confucian Zhongyong;
   Maimonadean distance equaled from extremes.
      Virtue must observe the mean. Aquinas said he did, Muhammed, too,
         immodest of their moderation.

Blonde's a dare. Be mine a middle color, neither dark nor fair.
   Not tall or short, fat or thin, at this middle station, midway,
      nel mezzo, my own perfect equation. Find brown compacted
         in the nuts of trees, the base beneath the oil paints, the umbers

and siennas; surprising in the sweets of chocolates and caramels
   and truffled beans. Softening the sacrifice of animals—
      tan their skins to brown, and brown by fire
         the bloody meat of fresh kills.

Let it temper the lust to browse and buy—
  who wants, even among the *middle* class, a suit or car,
    a tie or lingerie, or dinner plate, in medium brown?
      Brown's temper is melancholy, its rhyme a frown.

Red, yellow, and blue are tucked inside of brown,
  The mud of color, dirt of earth plus water: the planet's
    opaque watercolor. It holds antagonist and agonist,
      descends to the shit-brown leavings and compaction of the meal.

Brown sprouts cousins of deliciousness,
  mahogany and hazel, chestnut, rust and russet;
    from buff to bay to amber, fawn, sorrel, tawny, terra-cotta . . .
      but how to find a single word to paint the true medium?

To hold that mean between extremes?
  A seeker among very brown bears, one in search of proportion,
    civilization, fit, was one called Goldilocks, a thief
      driven blazing from a brown house into the darkened woods.

The Wives of the Poets

All poets' wives have rotten lives
Their husbands look at them like knives
    —Delmore Schwartz

The wives of the poets,
they never complain.
They know they are married
to drama and pain.

They know they are married
to more than their man.
They know there are others—
young lovers he can

fend off from the marriage
that keeps him afloat,
for rail as they may,
he won't rock that boat.

She won't read the poems
he's written for her;
the poems for lovers
will cause no great stir.

He knows she won't read them,
because her concern
is life (and not words),
but both feel the burn

of the daggers they throw,
the sharp looks that show
the rot in the lives
of poets, and wives.

The Up-Rolling of Time

When we escape middle age:

When the sun shines perpetual
And the floor no more needs waxing,
When the piles of papers don't pile up
And we are just relaxing,

When the pan never burns,
And the joints do not ache,
When the laundry is self-cleaning
And love is all we make.

When the brows' rows unruffle
And the hair sheds its gray,
When we can duck our duties,
We'll run outside to play.

When we escape old age:

When the sun shines perpetual
And walking is not taxing,
When we return to how we were
And waning conquers waxing,

When the spine's smooth and supple
And the rheum stays at bay,
When we can ditch our dentures,
We'll have no more to say.

When we grow a little smaller
And lose our breasts and teeth,
We will rediscover nursing
And diaper what's beneath.

When we grow smaller yet
And cells then re-cohere,
We will become as embryos
And, at last, will disappear.

Two-Part Song

Preserved Things

Of most things come and gone
remains little song—the milk got drunk, the egg got fried,
the bleached colors of the Polaroid lied. Moth wings
break into crumbs—parts don't add up to sums.
Yes, most things will slip and slide, eroding in the great elide.
I sing now of preserved things, of whorls in wood
and table rings; calico corn, gold and red,
like relic teeth in an ancient head;
ageless pussy willows in a glass, far from their lost river-pass;
an arrangement, too, of white
moonwort pods stretched tight like the papery
skin of a drum,
forgetful where they'd traveled from, yes,
all these things make a mighty sum.
To this, add things from the fridge, surviving on their arctic ridge,
a jar of pearl onions on a shelf,
a wishbone drying on the sill—probably it lies there still.
Let us add the things that freeze:
an ice age of meat and peas.
Yes, I sing a song
of things preserved: the parched, the pickled,
dried, conserved—inert but alive—unlike me,
they disdained to grow;
not dead, but changeless,
outside flow. The answer to a riddle
I wished not to know.

Things Thrown Away

To live is to scatter, even things
that matter, to send on its way
that which would stay. I am mighty,
lift crates, push boxes, flatten gates,
jettison the jetsam, float away the flotsam.
It's an art to lose it, Bishop said,
all I want is in my head, let photos curl,
let knits unpurl.
A collage I made, too long unseen—its cuttings
slot to magazines. The codfish from the freezer flies,
swims back to streams. The cat, the dog, both long dead,
Granny too, and what she said,
they leave a little heap of stones.
All may join in general decay, rosebuds
gathered when they may. The clothes
may soon fall to tatters, the roof crush a sinking wall.
I'd like to leave without a trace,
dissolve the lines that line my face, live lightly
on the dropping earth,
grow all compact and white and spare, a cube
of nothing, small and rare.
If I squeeze it small, it all fits there,
a rolling die in rarefied air.

Bounty

The fruit flies find our fruit, they slip
beneath the lid, a silver dome.
The dark fruit scent has drawn them in,
no other lures them out again.
They settle on apples, puckered figs,
they gorge in perpetuity,
may never fly back to their home,
(if they have ever had a home).
An allegory of choice? Well, yes—
in that we have no choice.
The fruit is fine, the day is long.
Let us feed, buzz, rejoice.

Page 18, "Nib Nok Nok": An imaginary language of rocks.

Page 27, "Holistic Practice": This poem is written in a nonce, rhyming stanza-form called "Rolling de Solas."

Page 36, "Bluish Animals": In his journal entry of February 21, 1855, Thoreau noted the scarcity of blue animals, a subject taken up by Louise Bogan in her 1936 poem, "Variations on a Sentence."

Page 47, "The Cornell Boxes": Joseph Cornell (1903–1972) was an American artist who created glass-fronted boxes with varying assemblages of objects.

Page 56, "Wertheim Park": Wertheim Park in Amsterdam is the setting for the annual Holocaust Memorial Day. During the ceremony, the rabbi sings a memorial prayer for those who died in the camps.

Page 68, "Hollandsche Schouwburg" was an Amsterdam theatre used as a deportation center during the Second World War. It is now a Holocaust museum.

Page 69, "Rotterdam Chiaroscuro": The epigraph is mine.

Page 73, "*Carnation, Lily, Lily, Rose*": A painting by John Singer Sargent (1886), depicting two girls playing with paper lanterns in an English garden.

Page 75, "Frozen Charlotte": A "Frozen Charlotte" was a widely popular nineteenth-century doll depicting a frozen, naked corpse. The Frozen Charlottes recalled several ballads, known throughout America and Canada, about a young woman who froze to death on the way to a county ball. The popularity of the ballads and the dolls marks the deep resonance the story had for North Americans.

Page 77, "In the Dark" uses the language of photography manuals.

"Page 86, "A Bit of Roof"": An umbrella.

SUSAN DE SOLA's poems have appeared in many venues, such as the *Hudson Review* and *PN Review*, and in anthologies, including *The Best American Poetry 2018*. She is a winner of the David Reid Poetry Translation Prize and the Frost Farm Prize. She holds a PhD in English from the Johns Hopkins University and has published essays and reviews as Susan de Sola Rodstein. Her photography is featured in the chapbook *Little Blue Man*. A native New Yorker, she lives near Amsterdam with her family.

ALSO FROM ABLE MUSE PRESS

Jacob M. Appel, *The Cynic in Extremis – Poems*

William Baer, *Times Square and Other Stories;*
New Jersey Noir – A Novel;
New Jersey Noir: Cape May – A Novel

Lee Harlin Bahan, *A Year of Mourning (Petrarch) – Translation*

Melissa Balmain, *Walking in on People (Able Muse Book Award for Poetry)*

Ben Berman, *Strange Borderlands – Poems;*
Figuring in the Figure – Poems

Lorna Knowles Blake, *Green Hill (Able Muse Book Award for Poetry)*

Michael Cantor, *Life in the Second Circle – Poems*

Catherine Chandler, *Lines of Flight – Poems*

William Conelly, *Uncontested Grounds – Poems*

Maryann Corbett, *Credo for the Checkout Line in Winter – Poems;*
Street View – Poems

John Philip Drury, *Sea Level Rising – Poems*

Rhina P. Espaillat, *And after All – Poems*

Anna M. Evans, *Under Dark Waters: Surviving the* Titanic *– Poems*

D. R. Goodman, *Greed: A Confession – Poems*

Margaret Ann Griffiths, *Grasshopper – The Poetry of M A Griffiths*

Katie Hartsock, *Bed of Impatiens – Poems*

Elise Hempel, *Second Rain – Poems*

Jan D. Hodge, *Taking Shape – carmina figurata;*
The Bard & Scheherazade Keep Company – Poems

Ellen Kaufman, *House Music – Poems*

Emily Leithauser, *The Borrowed World (Able Muse Book Award for Poetry)*

Hailey Leithauser, *Saint Worm – Poems*

Carol Light, *Heaven from Steam – Poems*

Kate Light, *Character Shoes – Poems*

April Lindner, *This Bed Our Bodies Shaped – Poems*

Martin McGovern, *Bad Fame – Poems*

Jeredith Merrin, *Cup – Poems*

Richard Moore, *Selected Poems;*
The Rule That Liberates: An Expanded Edition – Selected Essays

Richard Newman, *All the Wasted Beauty of the World – Poems*

Alfred Nicol, *Animal Psalms – Poems*

Deirdre O'Connor, *The Cupped Field (Able Muse Book Award for Poetry)*

Frank Osen, *Virtue, Big as Sin (Able Muse Book Award for Poetry)*

Alexander Pepple (Editor), *Able Muse Anthology;*
  Able Muse – a review of poetry, prose & art (semiannual, winter 2010 on)

James Pollock, *Sailing to Babylon – Poems*

Aaron Poochigian, *The Cosmic Purr – Poems;*
  Manhattanite (Able Muse Book Award for Poetry)

Tatiana Forero Puerta, *Cleaning the Ghost Room – Poems*

Jennifer Reeser, *Indigenous – Poems*

John Ridland, *Sir Gawain and the Green Knight (Anonymous) – Translation;*
  Pearl (Anonymous) – Translation

Stephen Scaer, *Pumpkin Chucking – Poems*

Hollis Seamon, *Corporeality – Stories*

Ed Shacklee, *The Blind Loon: A Bestiary*

Carrie Shipers, *Cause for Concern (Able Muse Book Award for Poetry)*

Matthew Buckley Smith, *Dirge for an Imaginary World (Able Muse Book Award for Poetry)*

Barbara Ellen Sorensen, *Compositions of the Dead Playing Flutes – Poems*

Rebecca Starks, *Time Is Always Now – Poems*

Sally Thomas, *Motherland – Poems*

Rosemerry Wahtola Trommer, *Naked for Tea – Poems*

Wendy Videlock, *Slingshots and Love Plums – Poems;*
  The Dark Gnu and Other Poems;
  Nevertheless – Poems

Richard Wakefield, *A Vertical Mile – Poems*

Gail White, *Asperity Street – Poems*

Chelsea Woodard, *Vellum – Poems*

www.ablemusepress.com